EXPLORE MY HEART

EXPLORE MY HEART
Velenda A. Mason

Printed in the United States of America

ISBN: 978-0-578-01489-0

Cover Design Concept: Velenda A. Mason

Cover Design Art: Isaac Mason

Contents

Preface

This book was going to simply be a collection of poems. As I read over the poems I decided I would incorporate the stories that inspired the poems. I always wanted an avenue to help teenage girls understand love and this book is an excellent start. Anyone who truly knows me, knows my desire to write. I want to spread the knowledge I have acquired on matters of the heart and mind. There will be many themes throughout *Explore My Heart*. Some chapters will have more reflective advice and detailed experiences than others. These poems will hopefully open your mind to the love experience.

I am in love with the idea of love. Love is one of the best experiences in life. Every relationship that I have been in has been a learning experience. I really want to fulfill two dreams at once by writing this book. This is truly an exploration through the stages my heart went through over a span of ten years. I want young women and men for that matter to read this book and have a better understanding of relationships. Understand that having high self-esteem makes a major difference in the decisions that you make in your life. One must truly love themselves in order to love others. My favorite saying is hindsight is always 20/20.

This book is a beacon of hope for anyone who loves writing. Do not let anyone tell you, you can not do something. I am a firm believer in what ever you put your mind to, you can do it. Every poem helped me when it was written. Writing is an expressive and therapeutic outlet and helps bring more focus to the thoughts swirling around in your head.

I want to thank all my ex boyfriends, without them this would not be possible, lol. I want to thank anyone who has ever read my work and been positive and encouraging. Thanks to everyone who helped read and edit if asked while I was writing. Thank God for allowing me to have the gift to write and express my views. Thank you to my parents, aunts, uncles, sister, brothers, nieces, nephew, cousins, and my grandparents. To all the friends loved and lost. Thank you to everyone who buys or reads this book. You have helped me actualize my dream. To my best friend who was always encouraging. You are truly missed and this book is dedicated to you. I Love and Miss You.

Chapter 1

That's Why I Love

He is special to me and always will be
It may not be true but he says he loves me
He's always there when in need
That's Why I love...
At times I may be mad or I may be sad
He comes along and makes me glad
I love being with him and being his girl
There's nothing else to ask for in this whole wide world
He shows me that he cares and always wants to be there
That's Why I love......
Our ideas are always the same
That's why I know this isn't a game
Forever we will always be. That's why I love,
        cause he loves me!

Do You Really Love Me?

Do you really love me is the question that I ask
Sometimes I think we entered this relationship too fast
You say you do but is it true
You don't show me by the things you do
We've been in this relationship for a very long time
And the whole time we were together I thought you'd
          always be mine
But now I see as time goes by I might be living in a lie
You know I love you I really do, why would I say it if it
          wasn't true
I would do anything for you in this world
All I really want to do is be your only girl
That would make me happy I'll make you happy too
But do you really love me and is your love so true

All I Ask For

All I ask for is a boy to make me happy
I want someone to be there to fulfill my needs
To be with me when I'm lonely and when I'm cold
Someone to be with when I grow old....
Not at this exact moment but to get started
I'm getting sick and tired of being broken hearted
I look very hard believe me I do
But I don't get the right one no matter who I choose
So either way you look at it, I lose
All I ask for is to have a companion in my life
A person who will in the future ask me to be his wife
I need that really bad but don't get me wrong I'll survive
At times I'd rather be dead than alive
Not because of boys but because of life.....
All I ask for is someone who loves me and treats me
      right
If I get what I ask for I hope it really last
Because going from boy to boy is in the past
Day after day, more and more
      I wonder if I'll get what I'm asking for.....?

The Things That I Give

I give too much and get nothing in return
Which to me has become a serious concern
Boys just don't know what they put me through
If I feel that I'm in love with you
There is no telling the things I'll do
I mean I'll still give to the man that I love
But give me something in return if only love
The things I give to you are special and some are mine
And all I need is a little of your time
So to whom it may concern please listen to my plead
Give me something in return give me something that I
       need

T hese were written about my very first everything (love, kiss, and lover). We had an interesting relationship from the beginning. Dorian was a very attractive young man so I had competition as far as people trying to suit him. This was the beginning when he first told me he loved me. His actions spoke louder than his words so I could not determine if the love was real or not.

I met Dorian when I was eleven years old and did not like him on first sight. He had the reputation of being a ladies man and I was not interested. His persistence paid off because I inevitably gave in. I truly fell in love with him and will always love him because he was my first. I always felt like I was giving him more in our relationship but he made me feel so special when I was with him. He was a great boyfriend despite the craziness.

Chapter 2

BEST FRIEND

My best friend and I have a true friendship
We could argue and fight but still everything would be
      all right
There are uncountable times to the fun we've had
And if we have many more I will be glad
Many times we don't talk for days
But if it was for a month my best friend still stays
We are different and the same in so many ways
That's why I know she will survive
To lose her would bring a tremendous pain to my heart
No matter what happens we'll remain friends forever
And at times you will always see us together
If she goes away which I hope she don't, the memories of
      her won't
Special she'll always be, because I consider her a best
      friend to me
She's a very strong person and she'll make it through
Because look who we're talking about it's my angel

Love,
Velenda Mason

Looking For That Light

I'm looking for that light to tell me where to go
That light of mine will teach me what I need to know
The troubles I've been through and go through each day
Come to me for a reason and some can't go away
I need that light wherever it may be
That light is watching and waiting for me
To guide me in the right places and not the wrong
I've been living in this world for such a short time
But I'm still looking for that light of mine
I live day by day sometimes thinking of the future
What will I be? Will I make something out of myself?
Do I have to pretend or can I just be me?
The world around me is something bad to see
I say that because all of my brothers are leaving me
Hopefully my light will show me all I need to know
And make sure I choose the right way to go
Looking for that Light is going to take some time
And looking will also be hard because the Light I'm
        looking for happens to be God!

A Star in the Sky

When someone dies they become a star in the sky
Since Angela went away there is not a day......
A day that goes by that I forget about her or what she
      meant to me
A star in the sky is where I'll know she'll be up above
      watching down on me
Right above my head, I don't feel that she's dead
It didn't really hit me and I don't know when it will
But I will always remember her as a star in my eye and
      I'm happy cause I know she's a star in the sky

I met my best friend Angela in the third grade. She was a year older than me but we were in classes next to each other. Our first encounter was in the lunch room one day. I had never spoken to Angela before, I may have just said hello in passing. So here we are in the cafeteria at different tables and I was talking to my friends and my mouth happened to be full. She just burst out and said stop talking with your mouth full. It was so funny because I was not talking to her and that day we became friends.

I always had friends with different backgrounds. I like to say I hung with both the cool people and the geeks. Angela was cool and rowdy so it made for an interesting friendship. I learned quickly that she was a great friend. We would clash at times because she was the boss and I do not like being bossed around. We were in the same fourth grade class and that made our friendship develop even more. I never had to worry about anything because I knew she had my back.

We loved reading books and formed our own book club. We collected money and everything so we could buy snacks for our meetings. We hung with a bunch of girls and formed a special bond because we did not want to participate in all the stupid stuff that girl groups go through.

We had the same classes except for sixth grade but were right across from each other. She would come home with me after school and we would do our homework and then hang out. We spent countless hours on the phone using three-way calling to trick people. We rode the train together when I moved to Maryland. We just had fun. We did have our moments when I wanted to punch her but she was a fighter so I had to think wisely about that.

She was the only friend who came to my house and slept over for the weekend. We had the best times even though she was often caught reading my diary. In the spring of our freshman year in high school she was killed. The poems were written as we waited for her condition to improve in the hospital. I had so much hope because Angela was tough.

I had been to church before but was not a member and I did not have a real understanding of the Lord. I lost all hope the day I got the call that Angela had passed away. I never cried so much in my life. The impact of her leaving so soon changed my life forever. It made me have a better appreciation for life and birthdays. It just made me different. She was too young to die but she was an exceptional young lady.

Chapter 3

If I Can't Be with You........

If I can't be with you, I don't want nobody else
Because you made me feel for you in a way I thought I
     couldn't feel
And you made me be myself and happy again
     At first we were friends and we formed to be much
         more
     And neither of us really knew what was in store
Your words and actions made me think and now I know
     why you stay on my mind
It's because I want you and only you, to be mine
If I can't be with you..........
     It's like living a life of pain
     Because I really want to be with you and want you
         to be my man
     And for you to be in love with me as long as you
         can
To be with you is what I really want to do because I
     never would have thought I'd have such strong
     feelings for you
     If I can't be with you at the present time, don't
         worry I'll wait
Because if it's meant to be we, will be together
I just wanted you to know that and I will always care for
     you
And I will always be there when you need me and
     remain a friend to you

The First Time I Saw You

The first time I saw you....I wanted you to be mine
And I knew that you would be in a matter of time
You came into my life and made me so happy inside
And every time I see you I have to smile
I miss you and the time that we shared
But I want you to know that I really do care......
About you and all the things you do
And the biggest thing of all is; I found that I love you
When I realized I did I couldn't believe it
The things you said to me and the things we would do
Made me fall in Love With You
Sure we have our problems like every couple do
But regardless of our problems I want to be with you
Once everything is over and we made the problems stop
You will really find out how much you have my heart

I Love You

In time you made me feel so good and you treat me right
You also make me happy and I like being with you
Those are some reasons why I Love You
Later in life I want us to be together because if I could
       make it that way,
I would Love You Forever
Often I think that I waited so long to be with you and to
       be held in your arms
And you gave that to me with your ways and your charm
Very few people can see why I feel for you the way I do
But they haven't been with you the way I have
And they haven't seen your smile or heard your laugh
Every time I'm with you or even if I hear your voice, it
       makes me want to stay with you forever and never
       leave your side
You stay on my mind a lot and that made me realize
       that you are the one who has my heart
Only you have made me feel this way and I constantly
       think of you everyday
Under any conditions if we are meant to be, we will be
       together happily
Any problems we have we will get through because if
       you love somebody that is what you do and I do
       Love You

Why I love Him So Much

Everyday this boy is on my mind, I think about him all
the time
It never use to be this way no one has made me feel this
way
Why I Love him so much remains a mystery to me
I do indeed love him; I love him with all my heart
I don't think nothing or no one can keep us apart
Some boys have been told I Love them but with him it's
different
I Love him so much that no one can be seen in my eyes
My eyes are stuck on him yeah that's how it is
He says he loves me so that really made me believe that
this isn't infatuation
When we are together we're in a whole different world
And deep in my heart I know I am his girl
No one else can really put a claim on me because
He's the one I Love and he's the one who loves me
I Love him on a level I have never loved before
He provides me with what I need and much more
Maybe he is the right one for me and maybe we are
really meant to be
He has touched my heart in a place where I thought it
couldn't be touched
And that is why I really love him so much

Without You

Without you there is no us
Without you there is no me
Because I Love you with all my heart
And you say you love me
Together we should always be
Without you makes me very sad inside
I can't be without you because
You are the twinkle in my eye
You make me feel as if I live in another world
And you mean more to me than any thing in this world
I'm your girl and you're my man
So to be without you, I can't quite understand
If I have to be without you I will not be with anyone else
Because I Love You and I want you for myself
If I can't have that then we don't need to be together
Because I don't want you part-time
I want you forever
Without you there's nothing else because if I can't be
        with you I'll be by myself
So if I can't have you, I'll wait until I can
Because the day will come when you'll be my man

A ngela passed away in May 1996 and I was a mess. Everyone around me tried to make me feel better but nothing can heal pain but time. Later that year I finally left the house and went on my first date. My date was a childhood friend who was interested in having a relationship with me. I was not really focused on him because it was four or five months after Angela passed. I was not emotionally ready for a relationship.

The day that I went on my first date a bunch of neighborhood boys were outside. One boy in particular was very inquisitive about my date. It was this young man named Darryl who I had met a few years back. When I first saw Darryl I was so smitten with him and I had never had a reaction like that so quickly for some-one. This particular day as he inquired about my date, he also asked for my phone number.

I was not sure if I was ready for a relationship but after talking to him more and more, I realized I wanted to be with him. I can not explain how this young man made me feel. I was so sad and he made me feel so good and happy. I was soooooo in love with him. I could not think about anyone but him everyday.

He made me feel so very special and called me his baby girl. Dorian was the only person I had loved, so Darryl was a breath of fresh air. Everyone knew I was his girl and he held me on the highest pedal stool. It was the greatest love.

Chapter 4

To Lose Someone You Love......

To Lose Someone you love can hurt you really bad
One day you're with your friend having a great time
But who would've thought it would be the last time
Making plans for the future and planning the fun you're
        gonna have
Then out of the blue she gets stabbed
It hurts you to know that your best friend might not last
All I can do is pray and say to God to let her be okay
Time went by and I was sure she would get a second
        chance at life
I was mistaken and she did leave
Of course all I could do was cry and grieve
So to lose someone you love can hurt you really bad
And my life will never be as it use to be because a part of
        me is gone
But I'll keep my memories until the day God calls me
        home

Peace of Mind

A long year this has indeed been
I need a good friend
Peace of mind is a state of being.......
It's something for some reason I'm just not seeing
Peace of mind is where I need to be
Haven't quite yet been
But still I need a friend
The mind, this time, money, violence, and crime
Hey! Where is that peace of mind
It's all within and yet I haven't begun to find that friend
Maybe I had it at one time
Yeah, I had peace with my mind
It's not here it's absent today, but what can I say
It's a state of being so how can I miss it
I do miss it
And my friend I can't seem to find is, Peace of Mind

The Source

My problems, these times, I'm looking for the source......
But yet I can't find
I am thankful for my life and for my parents' love
Could it be the source from up above
The source, you know, the one who makes the world go
   round
The source whom everyone is letting down
I lost my best friend and it hurt me extremely bad
But the source has to know the reason, know the reason
   why
Why it was my best friend who had to die
The source lets my heart rest and always remember that
   best friend of mine
Watching over me, throwing obstacles my way so I can
   be prepared for that day
That I meet the source
Ups and downs, people and life, there is much to
   sacrifice
Give unto others and others will give unto you
So one day I will see why things happen and who is the
   captain of the ship
Who will choose?
Choose who goes on his ship
The ship that we ride; with all the journeys that we all
   travel
Things will eventually fall into place and the source will
   make sure everything's safe

The End

Drugs, killings, money, people dying, children dying,
mothers crying
We are going to become extinct
I don't know when all this violence began
But when will we get to the end
Not the end of the world but to the end of these times
I'm tired of people dying, especially the ones I know and
love
So everyone has to get together and try to help...
If not for yourself, please help someone else
The end seems to be coming too quick and nobody is
making a change to prevent it
People are scared to lend a hand but as soon as
something goes down everyone wants to come
around
Don't wait until after, do things before they happen
The Black population decreases day by day and still we
can't find a better way....
To make people realize and open their eyes to the truth
It's a setup, Yes! It's all a setup, because whose killing
who
We are killing each other the white man isn't killing us
They put the drugs and the money there, and what do
we do
We use and abuse and our systems become immune
And the communities slowly disintegrate and if we don't
hurry it will be too late
I love my race and want all of us to be as one
But it will take hard work to get this done
So when did all this violence begin;
Don't know, don't care

Let's stop it before...The End

If Love Was Like

If love could be a simple thing would it really be worth
the trial?
If love was like a love song and took you to any level
possible and every time you heard those words, it
put you in another world
If love put you in a tranquil state of mind wouldn't it be
great to find
If love was like your favorite food and you could have it
everyday
Then after you were through with it you just threw it
away
Would you want love to be that way?
Like the sun shining right after a storm
When the weather changes from cold to warm
A love like that to keep you assured
Maybe love could be like a new pair of shoes
You don't want to wear them everyday but when you're
in the mood, would that be okay
Love is a feeling, a feeling you can't seem to control and
it's something you can't do by being told
You have to live through it, feel it, and become consumed
by the feeling
No one can tell you how to love and what to feel because
nobody can explain love for real.....
It's not a lesson; love does not come with directions
You have to give your relationships tests but you are in
no school and you may need tools.....
To fix it, your relationship that is
Finding love is a task that seems to require a lot of time
and may even boggle the mind
But what would life be without Love

If love was like an ocean and stretched out as far as the
       eye can see and every once in a while there would
       be a few waves
But wouldn't you want that if only for one day
The complexity of love makes it a high commodity
If love was easy and came with directions would it really
       be the same
What would love be without the fun and games
If we could love like Jesus loved,
Love would be like............That

I had found love with Darryl but still missed my best friend. During this time I started learning more about God and knew that I would see her again one day. I wrote what was on my heart at the time. I cried most times while writing but it was a good release. Losing her made me appreciate what I had with Darryl so much more. Angela was protective of me and I felt protected again when I was with Darryl.

I was in such a state while writing. I was feeling so many emotions because I was in love but my heart was still hurting from losing my best friend. I wrote *The End* because I had only written about love and there were a lot of things going on in the world. It was a tough time and my faith had been tested but I found that learning more about God helped. When someone close to you dies, it is a why game.

Why did she have to die? I had known people who had done terrible things but were alive and well. At fifteen years old you can not fully grasp losing a friend to violence. I had lost my roll dog and role model. Angela was a year older but very wise for her age. She was the only person I would take advice from but she respected my decisions. There were things that she would do that I did not agree with and vice-versa but we were always there for each other. From 1996 to the beginning of 1998; life was just hard.

Chapter 5

HAVE YOU?

Ever made love to someone you love
Ever had someone kiss you so intensely you want to stay
with them forever
Ever heard someone call your name while you are
making love
Ever looked into the man's eyes that you love with all
your heart, and know that you two will never be
apart
Ever had someone who does their best to keep you
happy
Ever had love in your life, a special love that can't be
broken no matter what happens to either of you
Well that's the reason for my little bit of
happiness, because I do and I have

Wrong Kind of Love

The best things in life are supposed to be free
If that is true why can't love be?
Looking for love is a hard thing to do and no one should
 look for love, it should find you
In my seventeen years of living the one thing that has
 been hard is finding love
Infatuation has hit me hard and my heart has no guard
 against....the pain I have endured
The wrong kind of love has made me stronger and has
 left my mind to ponder
No longer will I place my heart and soul in someone
 else's hands
My destiny, and my fate depends on me, not the love of a
 man
The wrong kind of love is what I fall for redundantly
If love is wrong for me, why is it I can't see
My eyes are wide open but yet they seem to remain
 closed
When they will open remains unknown
Not knowing whether or not someone to love will always
 be around
The wrong kind of love keeps me grounded but wears my
 heart down
If love can be wrong what can make it right
Is the price I'm paying worth love in my life?
Love cannot possibly be free because of all the pain,
 heartache, and frustration love has brought to me

A Long Journey

Traveling down the roads of life is quite difficult at times
The hardest part of this journey is deciding which one is
    mine
With God by my side there isn't anything I can not do or
    a height that I can not reach
I may not attend church but God is not a part of this
    search
I have found God and know where he stands in my life
This long journey has put me through many ups &
    downs
I have lost many old friends but new ones have been
    found
Could I say friends well it all depends
People who seem to be there and the ones who seem to
    care but if you really need them, are they really
    there
Family is what counts and the love that you receive and
    share....
With family at least you know that they aren't going
    anywhere
Life has no ending but a beginning each day
And you don't know where to go, God is guiding the way
A long journey I can't really say, just a difficult obstacle
    everyday

I Can't Take This......

When times were good and times were bad, I was there

When you claimed to be alone and said no one cared, I cared

When you were down and no one was around, I was around

I can't take this shi* you put me through I don't understand I've always been there for you

With all bad things you have brought my way, I thought I had the security that you would always stay

Times seemed to be pressed and my perspective has changed

Never can things go back to being the same

Why should I go through all this pain, why couldn't you find it in your heart to change?

I've changed for you and did things I didn't want to do and only did them because I Love You!

My love didn't touch you, it seemed to pass you by because never did you tell me the truth, you have always lied

Lied to me about trivial things and made my life hell and when I let you know all this, did you care-I can't tell

How could you possibly let I Love You come out of your mouth, it was never you but now your love that I doubt

I just can't find it in my heart to forgive you anymore

I can't take this shi* no more, I feel that I don't have to and since my feelings seem to mean nothing to you, there is nothing left to do, but Leave

I Have Forgiven.......But No More

I am a firm believer of "stand by your man" and I have
stood by you as long as I possibly can
I have forgiven you numerous times and all you seemed
to do was play with my mind, but no more
Our relationship has been to all extremes and us being
together was only a dream
Giving second chances is an understatement, I gave you
all I could and yet you still didn't take it
To give ones body, soul, and mind wasn't enough because
my heart you still did not find
Excuse me that was my mistake you found my heart and
my heart you did break
I have forgiven you and tried to right all your wrongs
and all the feelings toward you must now fall
I'm tired of being hurt and I don't want to endure this
pain, why did you have to play so many games?
I have forgiven you but no more, instead of going
backwards
I'm now moving forward

Scarred

My love for you was gained through fear
The abuse mentally and physically kept me here
Wouldn't let me leave every time I tried
You told me you loved me but yet you lied
These scars that are here are invisible to the eye, but
      they hurt real bad and I indeed have cried
Could you entering my life have been such a crime and
      you hurting me, this is your last time
I have been scarred for life by the pain you have caused
And do I regret it PAUSE......
I shouldn't have to think about it because you hurt me
      and that's no doubt
But did you ever love me is what I'm trying to figure out
My life was based upon you and you have just showed
      me what I need to do

I Have

I Have.......
Loved him, cared for him, stood by him, watched
    his back, received his slaps, punched him,
    kicked him, kissed him, held him, helped
    him out
I Have.......
Been there, never given up on him, changed him
    in a way, thought about him everyday,
    given six years of my life, even considered
    being his wife
I Have.....
In many ways supported all of his endeavors,
    whether they be good or bad, given him
    things no one else ever has
I Have......
Given my body as well as my unconditional love,
    given so much and only asked for attention
    in return, been hurt repeatedly-physically
    and in the mind

He Could......
Not give me any of the above and all I really
    wanted him to give me was LOVE

D arryl and I were in love but had our share of
      issues. Darryl and his son's mother were having
problems so in turn that caused problems in our rela-
tionship. While we were on pause I was talking back to
Dorian. I mentioned before that he was crazy and he
loved me but there were a few things we still had to
work out. I would not say Dorian was abusive but he did
hit me before and I ignored it because boys from the
neighborhood always played like that. I quickly learned
the difference between playing and actually being hit.

I was so frustrated and disappointed when I wrote
those seven poems. I had done everything I thought a
girlfriend was supposed to do. Ultimately, I decided that
he was no longer going to hit me for any reason and I hit
him back. Standing up for myself ended all the physical
abuse. I had heard of and witnessed him hitting females
before, but thought he would never touch me. I still
knew that he loved me but thought he had to hit me to
get the result he wanted.

I know people will say this to you and it may not
seem that important; Never let a spouse hit you. People
only do to you what you let them. As soon as I stood up
for myself, it stopped. Others aren't so lucky so it is
better to stop things before it becomes a cycle or esca-
lates. I stayed with him because he was my first every-
thing and he was a good boyfriend. His love for me made
him irrational sometimes but we worked through it.

When the poems were written I had found out
about him lying to me and I love myself too much to deal
with liars. No one is perfect and mistakes can be
forgiven but I could only take so much. Darryl called me
when I had just finished writing *Wrong Kind of Love*
and I read it to him and he was impressed. It was funny
because I was so nervous to read it to him but I did not
want him to think it was about him.

Dorian was a special person and you either loved or hated him. I spent a lot of time with him and so many people wanted him, I felt special having him. He had a difficult home life and not much luck in school so I did my best to make him feel that he was an important part of my life. I cared about him and did everything to show him but he wanted to have his cake and eat it too. Relationships are hard and at times I wished I would've stayed with him and worked things out. Some people who are from different backgrounds can not effectively make a situation last. We tried.

Chapter 6

Thank You

God has answered many of my prayers and the way that
    I repay him
I Keep the Faith
Believing in God and the Lord Jesus Christ has added
    guidance and direction to my life
With all the chaos and troubles in the world
God has the answer and is the only one who you can
    trust and turn to
When in despair don't doubt because he will be there to
    help you out
The one you can depend on, The one to help you out, The
    one who reassures you whenever you're in doubt
The inspiration behind your every move and thought,
    The one that guides you, The one beside you, and
    I want to say Thank You Lord

After the Storm

Losing someone close to you can really shake your faith,
    never thinking the one you lost is headed to
                a better place
It's taken years to understand and come to terms with
        the death of my best friend
A new found relationship with the Lord has showed me
        that after the storm you can live again
You have to be strong and keep the faith and never for
        any reason let the person be replaced

Missing Angela

Missing Angela is a hard thing to do
I try to move on and do things but I miss her all the time
I may see or hear something that makes her pop into my
    mind
I get jealous when I see others with their best friends
    and people do not realize how precious that is...
A Best friend
You assume you'll always be together and make plans
    and agree to be friends forever
But you never know when one of you will just up and
    leave
Visiting a grave for four years can really break your
    heart
You can not imagine the feeling and can never really be
    prepared for the depart

Rain

I am gentle, fragile even but that's not what I have
    everyone believin'
Yeah I act hard, and I act that way because I have been
    caught off guard
My heart has been left in the rain and no one has yet to
    make that claim
Has the past made me stronger or weaker?
Am I afraid of the commitment that comes with love or
    is it much deeper
You have to endure the rain to see the sun shine
And that's true but I have been through the storm and
    had lightening strike
And yet I still don't have contentment in my life

I remember going to church as a child and every now and then as a teenager. I always felt the need to understand God and the Bible better. My spirituality and faith was growing as I continued to write. Angela's grandmother was into church and Angela would discuss the things she was learning with me to open my mind more. When Angela was in the hospital I prayed and prayed. I also had so much hope. When she did not make it I was so upset and asked God why. Her grandmother gave me comfort at the funeral by letting me know she was in a better place and would hurt no more.

At fourteen that was the absolute hardest thing I had ever been through. I also believe that everything in life happens for a reason, God has a plan for everyone. With that being said I read this book about best friends a few years before losing Angela. The book was about a girl maybe ten years old and her best friend. Well one of the girls died and the other was absolutely devastated. She could not and would not function because of the pain she felt. I think I needed to read that so I could better handle the lost of my best friend. I knew that Angela would not want me to mourn forever because she was always pushing me to be the best.

I was so thankful to the Lord for allowing me to meet a friend like that. She set the standard really high and I could not find anyone to come close to our relationship. I also decided I would tell my friends and family how I felt about them while they were still here. I wrote in my diaries all about my relationships but not friendships. We had so much fun together and although I have the memories I would have loved to have everything documented.

Chapter 7

Us

If I told you I love you, would you say it back
If I want to commit to you, could you handle that
If all the promises I make are kept
Would that keep us together?
Would I have to follow steps?
Or would my devotion make us last forever
If I told you I would really change
Could we be together again?
Can you love me again, can things go back to being the
    same
You were more than a lover, you were my friend

YOU

It may seem that my feelings change like the weather
   but I always knew that we would always be
   something to each other
Maybe you entered my life at the wrong time, but a man
   like you I thought I'd never find
I have loved and I have hurt
You made me realize what love is worth
To live everyday knowing that someone has your back
Made me realize the qualities I lack
You have made my life stable
You made me visualize and actualize things I thought
   unable
You have made me happy but at the same time made me
   mad
We both were good for each other but also bad
This is an apology from my heart and even though the
   problems we have wont be erased this is a start
I reached out to you and opened my heart
And you took my hand
You were a friend to me, a confidant you seemed to touch
   my soul
You opened my mind and made me experience Love and
   Life, you helped me reach my goal
I now understand and realize I do not have to always be
   in control
You connected with me on a sexual level that I did not
   know I could reach
You not only showed me new things you took the time to
   teach...me that a relationship is give and take and
   that if you want to achieve success you have to
   forgive mistakes

The time spent triples the money and presents
I would rather have you more than any present
You have been in my life for almost two years and you
   stood by me so long that I erased most of my fears
My only fear now is how we will end
Will we ever get back together or will we just be friends
I LOVE YOU and at times I had my doubts and it took
   hurting us both for me to really figure that out
You will always be a part of my heart and mind
There is no way I could erase all the time...spent with
   you and spent in your arms
I want you to know despite all the bad I have done
I never really wanted to cause you any harm
I know that being with you has taken a toll on both our
   lives and that without each other we would have
   never realized how much we need one another
We may never be a couple again, but I will always be
   your friend
I reached out to you and you took my hand
You were:
My Friend, Lover, and My Man

T hese were written as a last resort for one of the best boyfriends I ever had. We had decided that we would go our separate ways but that was easier said than done. We had to literally hate each other in order to forgive and move on. He was the first boyfriend I stayed with longer than a year consecutively. We started as friends and that is why we are still friends til this day.

Our relationship was a bit hectic and in hindsight, I think I wasn't ready to be in such a commitment. He was so nice when I met him and made me feel relaxed. We instantly realized we were a lot alike. He was very nonchalant though and that upset me sometimes because I could not tell if he cared or not. A lot of our fights stemmed from him not talking about things.

He also was the first to completely spoil me. It's funny because everyone thought I was crazy to leave him, but I needed more than gifts. I was so confused during our relationship as well. Every other month one of my ex boyfriends would try to get back with me. I would in turn question my feelings for Kevin. We went through it and I should have treated him better. He did not deserve the treatment he received but my heart just was not ready.

The decisions we make are everlasting. I am glad that we are still friends because I do not know what I would do without him. We have our issues but he knows me very well and I need that. When I need advice or want to know if I am making the right choice, I normally turn to him.

Destiny Exits Nevertheless
No Illusion Substitutes

The heart can only endure so much
I loved one boy who took too much
By him taking, taking my heart
By him breaking, breaking my heart
It tore me apart
Haven't been the same since we split
When trying to love again, I seem to quit
The heart can only feel so long
I loved one boy, who loved me wrong
By him lying, lying to me
By him deceiving, deceiving me
It was the hardest thing for me to leave
Haven't loved right ever since
It seems that that love was meant
Realizing that his love was gone
Gone because he loved me wrong
My heart aches for the love received by him
All I want is for my heart to feel that love again
The heart can only take the pain
I loved one boy and my heart he drained
By him loving, loving quite well
By him throwing, throwing, I fell
I loved him so much and so hard
My heart aches, cries sometimes, my heart broke, it's
    still healing, he made me lose my feelings, my
    heart's torn because we are apart
Missing his touch, his scent, his lips, his sweat, his
    charm, laying in his arms, his physical and
    mental thought, his hands, mmm-missing that
    man

Missing my vision in his eyes
The heart can only begin to miss
I loved one boy who has me feeling like this
By him adoring, adoring us
By him ignoring, ignoring us
Leaving him was a must
Being blinded by his love, I gave him all my trust
Betrayal quickly followed
What was I to do?
Take break, lie, deceive, throw, and ignore too
Missing him wont set my heart free
Missing him, means missing me.

T his is my absolute favorite poem. I had been in rela-
tionships after Darryl and I parted ways and none
of them were right. When I wrote this it had been at
least two years since interacting with him. I had so
much trust and hope in him and our break up was such
a disappointment. It took so much to leave him and not
look back. I was literally sick and I could not eat. I had
become so weak I actually started vomiting. In that
moment I realized I had to get it together.

I wrote from my heart and although it was
therapeutic, I missed him. I missed the girl I was while
with him. I think that my boyfriends after him kind of
suffered because my emotions were all messed up. When
I first saw Darryl I knew I would one day be with him.
We had an instant connection and I did not know why, I
was in awe of him though. He was so nice and funny but
at that time he was taken so I kept it moving. He had
lied to my friend and told her that I had tried to talk to
him though, so I should have known that he was a liar
early in the game.

Love is truly blind because you see what you want
to see when you are or think that you are in love. When
he called me for the first time I was so happy and
excited. My year was not going well and he made me
smile for the first time in months. We spoke on the
phone for awhile and decided that we would meet up and
hang out on Halloween. There was always a haunted
house in the recreation center so I went to DC for that
and to visit him. We had such a good time and that night
solidify that we should be together.

We had a good relationship but as I mentioned
before he had issues with his child's mother and that
turned into drama. She was upset that we were together
and made it her business to break us up. My focus was
on him and the love that we shared and we made it
through the rough spots. He made me feel so very special

and you can feel that in the poem. The way that he looked at me and held me is unexplainable. Love conquers all if you let it.

For all his good, there was some bad. I realized after awhile he was lying to me about his relationship with his son's mother. I had reliable sources that let me know that he was not all he seemed to be. I confronted him finally because she knew information only told to him so I knew he was still talking to her. I had to leave him because I can not tolerate liars. I do not play second or other. I knew he loved me and his friends tried their best to convince me that he was not dealing with that female in that capacity. I had lost Angela and now I had to lose him and my heart was truly broken.

Chapter 8

Everything But.....

I can be their friend, I can be their lover
I can be this, that, and the other
I can be their Bit**, I can be their Ho
Why can't I be their girl is what I want to know
I'm good enough to talk to, I'm good enough to chill with
Good enough to cheat with, I'm good enough to Fu**
So why don't I make the cut
When times are bad, even hard I seem to be the one who
        always responds
I am the friend, the lover, this, that and the other
I am sometimes the best girl in the world
I seem to be everything but...their girl

My Sonnet 2000

Shall I compare thee to an empty glass?
You filled me up only to dump me out
You said you loved me but it did not last
It was never you but your love I doubt
Maybe a broken glass is more precise
The shattered glass cut deep into my heart
I gave you my heart and you ruined my life
When trying to love again, I can't even start
There were good times the majority bad
Loving you enslaved my heart and my mind
When we were finally over I should've been glad
Being with you wasted my love and my time
       So devoted was I, you were all I knew
       You taught me that love doesn't have to be true

I was a little upset, lol. I had been dealing with my ex-boyfriends as well as my male friends. Both were frustrating me and I could not take it anymore. Everyone would always have something to say about what I was doing and who I was doing it with. I did not have a boyfriend at the time but felt like I did because I was always being questioned. Some of the people who I had been talking to seemed to want more but never made the move. I have never been forceful in relationships and was not about to begin.

I had stopped dealing with Dorian and had to leave the love of my life so I was in a mood. The sonnet was written in my college English course and when the professor told us to write something I was stuck. I asked her if it had to be positive and she said "No", and that is what I came up with. It was a combination of not trusting people anymore and being disappointed because I had really tried.

It is nothing more frustrating than trying your hardest at something and failing. I was so comprising and determined and the two people I gave my heart to, crushed it. I found that being in a relationship worked out best for me though. I should have taken some down time between 1997-1999 because I was not emotionally stable.

If Not Him....Be Alone
I Love this man for the life of me I can't understand
Want to leave him but my heart won't allow me to go
Do I think I'll ever leave him, then my answer would be
       no
It's so hard because my heart is kept by him
I would leave him but I'll hurt more in the end
Every time I think about leaving I always begin to cry
I know he loves me but everything else seems like a lie
I ache for his love when he is not around
I hate his ass though when he's no where to be found
Loving him is so easy; trying to let go is so hard
I want to just place this situation with GOD
That's an easy way out so I want to do it on my own
I feel like if I can't be with him, I'd rather be alone

I Allow

Opening my heart was easy and now it's hard
I allowed myself to be hurt numerous times
I allowed men to play with my mind
People can only do to you what you let them do
And I have come to find that all love is not true
I want to have happiness and love at its purest form
I want LOVE and I want love to want me
I want to give all that I have and receive the same from
      a man
I'm not desperate though it may seem that way, but
      more frustrated with the journey
Love has taken a toll on my heart, my mind, my spirit,
      and my soul
Having Love then losing Love and wanting Love has put
      me in an emotional maze and I need to be saved

If You.........Understand

If you could understand that my heart is wounded and
    can only take so much pain
I want you to see, so let me explain......
If you could envision my view on love through my eyes,
    maybe you would understand why I fear and cry
I want you to appreciate and think about the things that
    I say
Understand and accept that I am stuck in my ways
If you knew that your affect on me has made me see
    what I want out of love differently
If you could step in my shoes and feel the pain that has
    hit me and traveled through to my bones and
    understand the reason why I am scared to be
    alone
You would empathize with my reason not to let go of
    what I have so easily
Not knowing whether you will provide the love that I
    need
Makes me hesitant and scared to leave what I know is
    guaranteed
You encompass all the qualities that I look for in a man,
    but until I know you
I keep that uncertainty
If you could assure me that I am entering this with my
    eyes wide open
And there would be no need for hoping while I am with
    you
It would alleviate the doubt in my mind and heart
If you could let me into your world and make me a
    significant part

I know that you can not predict the future and no
      promises can be made
If you could assure me that my heart will not be broken
      and I will experience pure and unconditional love
      with you
I will do what I have to, to make you Happy too

I was infatuated when writing *If Not Him Be Alone.* I was fighting for a relationship I knew was not good for me. I had met this young man John when my relationship with Rick was ending and thought it would be a better situation. This would be a lesson in the grass is not always greener on the other side. I never had a break in my relationships and that was not good for future relationships or my emotional well being. I am not sure what I was looking for but I did not find it with either boyfriend. I had fun but fun can only last for so long.

John was the total opposite from Rick and he made me laugh. I told John I couldn't go further than friends until I made up my mind about Rick. I finally decided I would leave Rick because I have a rule about cheating. If I have to cheat, I would rather leave and I left.

My relationship in the beginning with John was so wonderful. He had a son so I had to prepare for that. He told me if his son did not like me, we could not be together. I had to respect that and felt good because he cared about his child. His son was not that excited about me or our relationship. His son told me that his mother and father would get back together. I wasn't mad because a child should feel that way but the more time we spent together made us closer.

When I wrote *If You Understand* I was trying to explain to John that is was a difficult decision. He was a new person that I knew nothing about and I wasn't sure if I was ready to leave what I knew. I had my problems with Rick but we were approaching a year of being together so I wanted it to work. Ultimately I left Rick and started dating John.

Being with John was a learning experience. It made me trust again and we had a good time together. I also learned that everything that looks good, ain't good. There were many promises made on both ends but we are only human. I am glad for the experience.

Chapter 9

My Reply to Your Question 2002

To the man I love an answer to your questions
I can handle your intellect
Can you handle mine?
I have been waiting for the challenge for a long time
I am as stubborn as the next
You can try to compete but I am the best
At being an ass, I learned that from my past
I respect all that you do for me and your desire to be my
    better half and
I appreciate that we talk and laugh
If you are greater things, then yeah I will move on and
    let go
Because this experience right now I want to know...
How we will be for eternity
Will we love each other more than the heart can contain
I'm starting to realize without you would bring my heart
    its greatest pain
You are giving me what I want in life
Love, companionship, friendship, and time
 You have given me a peace of mind
Trust will follow because I love you so much and I don't
    want to be without you because You are.....
My life and you fill up all the space that has dwindled
    away at a fast pace
I know life is short and I want to spend every breathing
    moment Loving you
I want to love you until I can love no more
Tomorrow is never promised and you know I understand
That's why I will Love you for as long as I can

From Me To You

If I could put into words the things I want to say
The feelings I would like to convey
I have loved and been loved
Be it right or it wrong
Be it short or it long
Not quite this way, not all day everyday
With each day that passes the more I wish my LOVE
      last
If I could put into words the way you make me feel
When I think about the possibilities I'm scared of the
      real
Happiness scares me but you make me feel safe
Your feelings for me put me in an unfamiliar place
Don't like to plan for the future because then I feel the
      need to run
But you do or try to make every second fun
A wise man once said Ride This Until the Wheels fall off
Well Baby I'm ready for the ride as long as you are by
      my side
In a short time we have been to each other what I think
      is hard to find
You are my friend, my lover, and my man and I want us
      to make this work for as long as we possibly can
If I could say to you the things that are in my heart and
      mind
And have you understand I am not use to a GOOD MAN
I am not willing and I am not going to lose you because I
      have a fear
The only words that I can say to let you know how I feel
      today would be I KNOW I WANT YOU HERE

My doubting, pouting, and crying are all emotions that
    are normal emotions that I feel for men
But thinking of you and us I don't want to go back to
    where I've been
You may indeed be what I have prayed for and so much
    more
I can only look forward to the things we have in store
The fights or disagreements that we have are just stones
    in the road we have to pave
What we feel for each other we must save
Times will get rough, I'm sorry will not be enough
Anything worth having is worth fighting for and it may
    get tough
Just think about the good times shared and f**k the
    petty stuff
If I can put into words how we went form sex to making
    LOVE
When you touch me I know that your arms are where I
    am supposed to be
I LOVE IT when you make LOVE to me
To Kiss you, Hold you, Feel you gives me an emotional
    rush
All the extras you do, hmm well that's just a plus.......
    There is just so much to US
I just want you to see me the way I see you
And understand that these feelings I have for you make
    me do the things I do
I would not allow myself to feel but so much and now
    that my heart has been touched, I don't know
    what to do
All I want to do is LOVE you
I want to make you happy, I LOVE to see you smile
Even though our stubbornness almost made you walk a
    mile..........
All the problems just make us stronger and able to
    endure each other longer

If I could be any where in the world
With You is where I want to be
I am safe, happy, and content
And as the days go by we will see if this LOVE is
        meant..............
TO BE

Can You? 2003

Can you be the man that I need in my life
Can you fulfill my dream by one day making me your
    wife
You know what I want and you know what I need
Will you be the one who will make it seen
Can you be the man to renew my faith in love

Can you make it so my heart no longer hurts
Are you the one for me, can I end my search
Can you make it so that if I shed another tear
It will be only tears of happiness because you are here
Can you make me feel the way I know I should

Can you make the past I've had be worth it all
If I was to trip again would you let me fall
Can you be the one to chase away my fears
Make me feel really loved after all these years
It may seem sudden and there is no rush
I want you to be on the other side of us

I want you to continue the things that you do
I want you to know that my final decision is to be with
    you
I want you to know that I'm glad you're in my life
You make it easy to want to love again
I'm glad you're my lover as well as my friend
Can you be all the things I want......... or do you think I
    am asking too much?

You & Me

When you think of life without me
How do you really feel?
Finding true love is very hard and what we have is real
Forgiveness and hurt are on the road to Happiness
People make mistakes.... We have made mistakes
We will probably continue to make mistakes
You are not the only one who has been hurt
I don't know how much you think love is worth
I am willing to go another round
You can win the fight if you don't fall down
When you think of life without me
You can think of what you'll miss
But when you think about life with me
It's worth all of it
We have so much good and it surpasses the bad
I do not want to live thinking of what we could have had
I want US to be together and work it out till the end
I can not and refuse to be Just a Friend
We are friends and that's what makes us strong
I do not want us to move on
I want us to stay together and continue to grow strong
When you think of life without me
A smile will leave your face
I am a part of your heart and that you can not replace
When you think of life without me...but wait you can't
      because you cannot be without me...this is Fate

Now I Realize

I never thought that I would regret
I definitely thought he'd forget
We were given a second chance
But God has another plan
I need that closure or that chance
To experience who I think is the purest man
Out of the field of flowers, he chose this rose
I could've fought harder because I knew years ago
But I didn't and I let him go
If it's meant, we'll meet again and if we are never lovers,
     I just hope that we can be friends
He was there for me and knew a side which I now hide
If we are brought together again....I just need him, I
     Miss My Friend

There were a mixture of emotions when dating John. We had such good and bad times with each other. At one point I really thought we might marry. We discussed getting married but not knowing his history would hinder our relationship. As I mentioned before I hit it off with his son, so that barrier was out of the way. John had a way of making the details of his past a little unbelievable. Since I met him at a store I had no one to reference and had to take his word for it.

Two of the poems above were in response to poems that he had written me. We communicated very well and I guess putting words on paper only helped. John truly made me laugh though and I needed that. We spent so much time together and discussed moving out together but I felt something was not right. There were many things that made me question some of the things he would do.

His job had unusual hours so I think he used that to his advantage sometimes. I can sincerely say that we were in love at one point but things went wrong. He was my second longest relationship so we fought hard. Some things just aren't meant to be and it is best that we parted ways. He was sneaky and lied a lot and since I absolutely can not stand liars, we just could not work. It was upsetting because we were together for a while but I had to be strong and move on once again.

Chapter 10

Step

Step into my shoes and look through my eyes for one
      minute of one day
Then what will you have to say
So many judge or assume
But they could not be me for a minute
I am strong
I am wise
I am what you despise and try to disguise
I am too much to handle because I have standards
That are hard to meet
I am so damn truthful I'm surprised I still have my teeth
If I knew that life would be such a challenge
I would've let you wear my shoes

Today Not Too Soon

Do I only miss what is not there?
Because once I have, I do not want
Why do I put up such a front?
I need one friend who will always be there
I need one person to show me they care
I want to feel that all the pain I have suffered
Will sooner than later become my buffer
My heart has been through so much
And all I want is for that one person to touch it and heal
       my wounds
And if he comes today, it won't be too soon

Fog

Love is difficult
But who said it would be easy
I find myself wanting what I never had
I find myself needing love so very bad
Why?
I had both parents and love from each side
Why is it that I choose to hide?
Maybe because at one time I was told I was not cute
At one time it was thought that I would do nothing with
      my life
Once before I was taken advantage of
I was abused
I took many hits, been called a Bit**
Been asked to snitch
Been the cause of drama
I am hated by plenty of baby mama's
Love is difficult
But at times it seems worth the trial
Because if I can have any amount of happiness, I can
      wait a while
I have been lied to, cheated on, beat on, betrayed some
      things I rather not say
A lot basically has made me question my worth
I have loved and lost
Lost my Best friend
How can you begin a life when it always appears to be
      the end?
With all the bad there has to be some good
I know when someone loves you it is just understood
There are various reasons to make me feel unloved
Then I started to understand and talk to the Man above

That has helped me more than I could ever know
I always turn to him no matter what the cause, and God
      put me on a path when I was lost
I need love because I guess it gives me purpose
It gives me the will to live
I really want to have kids
To actualize a product of love from myself, that will be
      something else
I had a home, two parents, brothers and a sister, a lot of
      friends, boyfriends, aunts, and uncles
I did not have it too bad
But receiving the wrong love has distorted my view
How can someone else love you when you don't know
      you?
I have altered so much for so long I do not know what I
      want or where I belong
Who am I?
No one has seen the tears; no one has heard me cry
I smile on the outside while I die inside
If I find me and be me then love will love me
I guess it is worth the ride

Mother

Many times you have been there for me, whether it was
  to lend a helping hand, making me understand,
  financial help and advice; you are the force in my
  life
Only a wonderful woman such as yourself would be so
  generous and selfless
Too many times you have asked for things and been
  denied, but yet you push on and put your worries
  and troubles behind
Having you as a mother is the greatest gift on earth, you
  always try to keep your children from being hurt.
  You make me live and you make me proud
Every time I see you I am happy, because I see you in
  me and to have any of your traits is an honor to
  me
Regardless of what goes on in my life I know you are
  there and what more could a daughter ask for...?

If I do not tell you enough how much you mean to me
  this is my declaration
I Love you More Than you know and I want to thank you
  for helping me grow
You are my life and the reason why I am here
I live to make you proud, everything I do is because of
  and For You!
You are a Mother in Every way and despite what you
  may think you are a Wonderful Mother Every
  Day.

I was trying to figure out what part I played in the failure of my relationship. People always had something to say about the choices I made and I was tired of hearing it. I believe in learning by doing, it's not always a happy ending but life is not always a happy ending. It is very frustrating having people questioning everything you do and I was tired of it.

It was also hard to pretend to be happy all the time when inside I was hurting. Everyone would think I was the toughest partly because that is what I portrayed. It still sucks when I do not want to be bothered and no one can understand that. I need a day off sometimes and it is not the easiest thing to do when people are always in your face. I guess it's a gift and curse. Sometimes I am thankful that people take a liking to me but it gets to be too much when everyone wants all my attention.

One of my mantras is I don't have regrets because most things were thought out before I did them. When I wrote *Today Not Too Soon* I was thinking about one boyfriend that I should have kept. Donte was the sweetest boyfriend; I met him in the sixth grade. He was so in love with me from the day we met. There were a lot of other things going on so we did not get a chance to actually be together until later. Dorian was so jealous and went out of his way to keep us apart.

Our dating, if you want to call it that was so funny. We had the best times and I should have handled our relationship better. As I always said if it was meant to be, it will be. He was so attentive and just let me be me all day, everyday. I actually ran into him years later but neglected to get his number so I lost him yet again.

Then I wrote my mommy that poem for mother's day. We had an interesting relationship because I did not understand the things she did until I was sixteen. I always felt like my mom listened to my dad too much. When we finally had to live alone we grew closer. Now she is my bestest friend. We don't always see eye to eye but we have a great relationship.

Chapter 11

Fourteen

Words cannot explain what I would like to convey
I love you and have been for 365 Days
And I plan to continue.........
We embarked on this journey not knowing what the
    future would hold
I don't regret a second, a minute, or a day
No matter what has happened in the past I love you
    anyway
We have hurt each other and brought so much joy to one
    another
When I think about my future I think about no other
All the pain has made us stronger
The love we share will keep us together longer
It seems like we have been together for years
And we are...
Everything that Love should be.....
We are we

I Would....

I would Love to be with you for the rest of my life
I would Love to be your Best friend as well as your wife
We could be so much to each other
But we let our egos and pride smother
All the good and we have had so much
So why is it so hard for us?
I would Love to help you raise your son
I was never for kids, but you made me want one
I mean two because I already care about yours
We could be the epitome of Love
If we let ourselves Love freely
I Would..........If You Could

I Am Willing

I am willing to overlook what I see as dangerous
I am willing to do that because I want an us
I am willing to change so our love can remain
I love you and it's worth the pain....
I have been going through to be with you
Time away made me want to stay
Your love for me should be enough
I worry too much about the small stuff
I am willing to be the woman you need
You deserve that because you are a King
My king, whom I adore I'll do my best not to hurt you
    anymore
I gave you my heart in exchange for yours
And I know with your love, you'll heal the sores
We are meant to be I love that we're a We
You are a part of my heart as well as my soul
We belong together so I've been told
I love You so much and don't want to live without your
    touch
You fulfill my life, changing my ways is a small sacrifice
If the price is to one day be your wife

I Thought.......

I thought I met my husband the other day
But he just turned out to be a nigga from around the
        way
But I looked again because he reminded me of a friend
I thought I had found love at its purest form
Now I realize I had the norm
I could swear he was my husband because he had all the
        qualities that my husband has
I had to run back because I looked too fast
All the men of the past and all the hurt that came with
All disappeared because of this man's lift
He was so special and appeared to be true
But it seemed like a blur
Damn I almost had him couldn't really catch up
It's a bad thing when love fu**s up

I'm the Last to Know

I went from good to bad and sometimes I wish I never
    had
I'm living by what happened with my Mom and Dad and
    I find myself mad
I gave my all and always came up short and I don't know
    what else to do
Can Love Be Taught?
Patience is coming, I am learning to be patient but with
    trying to find the man for me, I am tired of
    waiting
While I am trying to be committed and give my all to
    prevent that call that I don't want to make
I end up leaving for my own sake
I am always the Last to Know......
When my man is being deceitful and lying
I don't know what to do because I am tired of crying
I am content with being unhappy because I don't know
    what happiness is
I don't know what happiness is
I don't know what happiness is

The Girl Has Left the Building

As of Today I officially give up. I have tried to Love on
several occasions and all has failed. I am tired of
tears and tired of games and I ask myself who is
to blame. I have given until I can't give no more,
and a man in my life is kinda a sore....on my
heart because the feelings have officially stopped.
It's not worth the pain and heartache I refuse to
shed another tear. I question my judgment.
Why am I really here?
If someone had told me love would be this way, I
wouldn't have leapt into it at such an early day. I
started early and it made it cold,
Now I'm feeling the same way while loving old. It
shouldn't be this hard to have happiness in your
life and people shouldn't treat you like you are
their wife.
I will not be a second and I will not be the main
If I cannot be the only then I'm officially out the game

T hese final poems were written at the end of my relationship with John. I was more disappointed in him than hurt. I believed in and trusted him even when I knew I should not have. I learned a valuable lesson from my experience with him. I am always thinking that in order to get over somebody I must move on fast. I put myself in that situation with John and felt really stupid in the end. But what can you do?

There was too much bad blood for us to remain friends although I think we attempted. I learned that you should always go with your gut. Of course everyone is going to be on their best behavior in the beginning, it's the middle you have to worry about. I learned to slow things down and really try to get to know someone before entering a relationship.

The Girl Has Left the Building is the truth. I felt at times I may have been the main girl, never second, mostly only. I always use to say to my boyfriends if you cheat and pull it off, you are good. I do not mean it in a congratulatory way but I am so observant and inquisitive; so to pull it off would make for congratulations. I still feel that way though and always will. I want what I want when I want it. I do not like to play games. There is no need to cheat on me, because the door to leave is always open.

Chapter 12

I have been lucky in my fourteen years of dating to experience real love more than once. It is a beautiful experience and I would not trade it for the world. I want young men and women to learn the difference between infatuation and love. It is a job and it takes compromise and sacrifice but it is well worth it. I have gone through enough in my lifetime to know a thing or two. Just know that with faith anything can happen.

I could have let all the negative things that happened in my life make me bitter but I did not. Every experience is about growth. It has taken me awhile but I finally realized that people can only do to you what you let them. I have learned to be very patient and not to judge a book by its cover. Another mantra I love is; everything that looks good ain't good. With that being said, I have to stop being shallow. I am sucker for a pretty face and that leads to heart break.

I know one day I will meet my match, better half, and best friend. I know what I want from a man and it has taken a lot of bad seeds to figure it out. I want a love that knows no boundaries. You have to understand that love does not mean changing who you are. If you feel changes are needed to maintain then that call can only be made by you. I have also learned not to sweat the small stuff. At the end of the day you can come home to somebody or come home alone. I would rather come home to somebody.

Also appreciate your family and friends while you still have them here. You really do not know when you will see somebody for the last time. It is a terrible feeling to think of all the things you could have or should have done. Besides you are going to find a small amount of people who genuinely care about you and your well-being.

Every person you meet will affect your life. You have to decide whether or not people are keepers. I would rather have five true friends, than fifty fake ones. Friendships should be reciprocal. Never let anyone take advantage of you for any reason. Friends will be there through good and bad times. If you have to keep a tally of things that a friend has done for you, then they're probably not your friend. Angela set that standard really high and I did not realize that until eleven years later.

Life is truly what you make it, so live it to the fullest. Love is wonderful so open your heart to experience it. Put God first, it is better to have something positive to believe in than nothing. Get to know the Lord it will make you a better person. It does not hurt to have guidance and someone to look up to. When life gets to be rough having someone to turn to no matter what, is the best.

Love yourself because no one can love you like you can. I have found that having high self esteem will make you succeed in ways you can not imagine. Men will tell you all kind of things to get what they want but when you love yourself it is a little harder for the tricks. If people do not believe in you show them that you can stand alone. I was grateful to have teachers who cared about me so I wanted to do my best to live up to their expectations. Striving for excellence can never go wrong. You should always try new things. The worst anybody can ever tell you is No. Setting goals high only means that if you fail to reach the top, you will still be doing well.

Surround yourself with positive, motivating people. When everyone is reaching for the best it will only drive you more. Dream, Dream, and Dream some more. I am writing this book because I wanted to fulfill a dream. Dream complete.

www.ingramcontent.com/pod-product-compliance
Lightning Source LLC
Chambersburg PA
CBHW051838040426
42447CB00006B/585